T. A. Acker, LLC
13 Lagan Lane
Port Wentworth, GA 31407

Acker, T. A.
Why Men No Longer Chase
ISBN: 978-0692282434 (T. A. Acker, LLC)

WHY MEN NO LONGER CHASE

T. A. ACKER

T.A. ACKER, LLC

I dedicate this book to those
who are willing to see themselves
within the pages.

Special Thanks

Erica Acker
Teia Acker-Bynes
James Jenkins, Jr.
Calvin Jones
Toni Jones
Devin Thomas
Tiffany Thomas
Melissa Walthour

Your input on this book project is priceless.
Much love and appreciation to you all.

TABLE OF CONTENTS

INTRODUCTION   3

I. THE VERBAL CHASE
Chapter 1: *Chase* is not clearly defined   9
Chapter 2: The chase is too blurred   17

II. THE MENTAL CHASE
Chapter 3: The chase is too unfamiliar   29
Chapter 4: The chase is too familiar   35
Chapter 5: The chase is too intimidating   41

III. THE PHYSICAL CHASE
Chapter 6: The chase is too unrealistic   51
Chapter 7: The chase is too superficial   61
Chapter 8: The chase is too exhausting   65
Chapter 9: The chase is too uncertain   71
Chapter 10: The chase has too many runners   75

IV. THE DIGITAL CHASE
Chapter 11: The chase versus technology   81

V. THE SPIRITUAL CHASE
Chapter 12: The chase versus character   87
Chapter 13: The Summation of the Spirit   93

ABOUT THE AUTHOR   101

WHY MEN NO LONGER CHASE

INTRODUCTION

Consider this story: One man and one woman sit opposite of each other at a table. Each one is given four coins (a penny, nickel, dime, and quarter) and four bills ($10, $20, $50, $100). The man is given all of his currency with the front-side down (tails), while the woman is given her currency with the front-side facing up (heads). They study their respective currency for 10 minutes. They are not allowed to flip the money over to the opposite side. After ten minutes, the money is taken away from both of them. A neutral person begins to ask the both of them questions about the money, only based off of what was present on the bills or coins (no numbers, or mentioning of names of the men on them).

As a result of this little experiment, the man is able to answer questions based off the places and things that were placed on the back side of the money, because that's all he saw, studied, and remembered (i.e. the names of designs of buildings, or significant events in the picture). The lady was probably better at answering questions about things on the

3

front of money (i.e., placement of serial numbers, the kind of tie worn by one of the Presidents, the direction they faced, etc.). It's because she only studied the front side and saw such detailed things. Unless they shared what they knew individually to each other, they only will know what they learned separately.

It is important to know that despite their studying opposite sides of the same money, the value of the money didn't change. The penny was and still is valued at one cent. The dollar bill with Benjamin Franklin is still worth $100. Nothing changes the value. Although we spend money all of the time, we may not always know which bill has the U.S. Capitol on the back of it, or which coin has the eagle. To many, those details are never relevant. The point of this is to illustrate perception—but not just what we see, interpret, or understand, but also the perception of those who stand opposite of us and are affected by what we say or do. When it comes to the subject of love and the pursuit of it, perception plays the same role. Love is love, and loses no value as it stands, but is always viewed from two different perspectives - man and woman.

With that being said, the purpose of this book is to show how both men and women play a role in the subject of "chasing" and why both sides affect it in positive and negative ways. I am no expert at love, nor am I a psychologist specializing in relationships between men and women. But I am a man, and I remember those instances when pursuing someone didn't work for my benefit and was left feeling less than worthy. That feeling affected other "pursuits" that I attempted afterwards. On the other hand, I also can recall those instances where my own ignorance, arrogance, and pride caused relationships to sour and end. I am sure that you, the reader, can recall similar situations, or you may be going through those moments now.

We all have observed moments by our friends or family members that led to thoughts and opinions about love that we hold true even to this day. Observations of other people's behavior and attitudes about the pursuit of love also prompted my interest in writing this book. I have noticed, on many occasions, people downplaying the word "chase" as it pertains to attracting and initiating contact with someone. There were men saying that they would rather "chase their liquor" (meaning to buffer it with another drink) than to chase after a woman. Some women expressed how much they liked a guy, but they refused to chase after him. I am sure they have strong, valid reasons for thinking those thoughts (or maybe they do not), but I always wondered what prompted those thoughts in the first place. I also wondered how much men and women think their respective viewpoints are correct and without flaw.

Equally important to knowing what this book is about is what I don't want this book to portray. This book is not about *pointing the finger* or *blaming the man for everything*. Yes, if a man is pursuing a woman, he must have some attributes that interest her, but there are some aspects that only she can control as a woman. There are reasons to the whole "chase" process that are presumably provoked and controlled by women, so the end results are not solely on the actions of men.

Please understand that this book is not about *exemption*. A man who wants to attract a woman should not receive a pass from being a respectable and mature person or simply thinking like one. This book isn't *anti-pursuit*. Men have been known to initiate the so-called "chase." But, both men and women have a role to play in how the "chasing" process succeeds or fails. It is affected by the mindsets and actions of both sides.

I kindly ask that you consider the viewpoints of the opposite sex, that you are honest with yourselves, and that you accept the truth about yourself if apparent. Don't stress yourself over past instances when reading, but graciously accept the lessons learned from those moments. I hope that my words and thoughts are able to spark discussion among readers and influence great decision-making in how men and women interact in their pursuit of friendship and love.

I thank you for taking the time to read *Why Men No Longer Chase*. Feel free to discuss and share your thoughts on social media by using the hashtag, *#WhyMenNoLongerChase* in your comments. I look forward to seeing them! Enjoy!

- T. A. Acker

I.

THE "VERBAL" CHASE

Chapter 1

Chase is not clearly defined

Are you transitive or intransitive?

If you look in any dictionary, you will find the definition of *chase* to be similar. As a noun, the word simply refers to the *pursuit* itself or the object that is being pursued. But if we looked in-depth at the verb tenses of the word, we may find something very interesting. (If you are not a fan of grammar, this next point may seem very boring to you.) In most dictionaries, when a word is described in a verb tense, you have two types: transitive and intransitive. Transitive verbs are verbs done to someone or something (direct objects), while intransitive verbs do not contain direct objects. For example, let us take a look at the following sentences:

He *plays* guitar. (*Guitar* is the direct object, making *play* the transitive verb.)

He *plays continuously*. (There is no direct object here, so *play* is now an intransitive verb.)

Now, that you are thrilled to know the difference, here is where I relate both versions to the word, *chase*. The transitive definition could mean to follow someone with the hopes of attracting, winning or gaining something (i.e. friendship, relationship, and/or marriage), while the intransitive definition could mean to follow in pursuit. Who or what is being pursued is not specifically mentioned. This gave me some reason as to why men and women disagree on the "chasing" aspect. Some people specifically know what they want, and because they know, they will only pursue that. On the other hand, some folks begin a pursuit without the object in mind, clinging to the hopes that the pursuit itself will reveal that object to them.

Chase vs. Court

To *court* someone, by definition, means (transitively) to seek the affection of that person. Another explanation can take this definition a step further in saying that *court* means "to seek to win a pledge of marriage from." An intransitive definition refers to the "engaging in social activities that can lead to engagement and marriage." (By this, I am referring to the telephone calls, the love letters, "I miss you" text messages, and the dating.) From an animalistic standpoint, the word means to perform actions in order to attract the opposite sex. Without diving into the conversation of our animalistic nature as humans, it is easy to draw similarities in how males and females interact.

Both sides have a role to play in bringing a potential relationship into reality. As adults, it is not enough for many men to feel that if he "chases," he'll get the woman of his dreams, she'll immediately fall in love with him, and they will live happily until the end of time. That sounds easy, but not always true.

If men operated solely from definition, *courting* a woman is more fulfilling than *chasing* a woman. The two terms are not as interchangeable as we may think. When *chasing* a woman, he expels all of the energy pursuing her (unless she is running, which will be further discussed later). Thinking back to all of those cartoons from childhood, the character doing all the chasing was usually the one being duped, spun around, and/or punished for chasing what was enticing and admirable. The character on the other end of that chase was smart enough to know that regardless of was said or done, the energy stored was in his/her favor, and all of the energy used was from the chaser. If a man feels that a chase is more of a risk than a benefit, it will be difficult convincing him to *chase* after the lady he wants.

Instead of trying to convince him that chasing a woman is the best move, introducing the concept of courting each other proves more valuable. As much as society paints a bad picture in how men act in relationships, how men stray from commitment, how men are "dogs," and so on, some of the criticism displayed can be simplified down to a matter of perception and definition. If "courting" someone means giving a piece of oneself to someone that will give a piece in return, relationships can appear more balanced, more cohesive, and more unified. It is within a man's psyche that he wants to show strength – mentally, physically, etc. If he "chases" and loses, he may feel defeated and rejected, but if he courts and is courted in return, he feels a balance. Even if the situation fizzles and goes away, at least he would not feel as if he was the only one who gave emotions, time, resources to the building of a long-lasting, loving relationship. (Okay, maybe not at first, but eventually he'll think that.)

Chasing is usually a unidirectional method. One person is the dart and the other person is the bull's-eye on the board. The board is never thrown to meet darts, but vice-versa. The darts are thrown in the direction of the board, with hopes of making contact accurately. Relationships between people are no different. If a woman feels she should be "chased," then she is asking the man to "throw" himself at her, and maybe he'll make contact. If he doesn't, he'll just fall to the floor with the other "darts" that didn't stick, and she, as "the board" will remain mounted high in her position, awaiting the next dart—excuse me, the next man (unintentionally or intentionally). Courting is not the same concept.

Courting is not a dart-and-board situation. This process is like lemonade. Men can be the lemons, and women can be the sugar, and the water in the pitcher can represent their relationship. If the water is full of lemon, and not enough sugar, it is too sour. If the water is full of dissolved sugar, it is sweet (perhaps too sweet), but still has no distinct flavor. But when the right amount of lemon meets the right amount of sugar, then the beverage is perfect. It is about being complementary. Men don't chase anymore because many have reached the maturity level that, instead, prefers courtship.

Selfishness

Consider this statement: *"I don't know what he sees in her. He can do better than her."* Many men have heard this before, either directly or indirectly. For some time, I have wondered why such a statement is said in the first place. Ponder on this point: a woman says those above statements to a man, and as he reflects back in time, he remembers something important. There was once a time when he was possibly chasing after this same woman speaking these statements. He pursued her only to be rejected. He didn't forget that moment. Yet, in the present, he has to hear and feel those statements from that same woman?

In his mind, the man is now wondering a few things. First, did she like him and simply didn't say anything? Secondly, is she jealous of the man's current relationship with someone else? Thirdly, does she now realize her window of opportunity closed? Instead of saying he could find better, why didn't she try to be the "better" person? She doesn't really want the man, but doesn't want to picture him with anyone else. As much as women want to be chased and pursued, sometimes it takes having a mature stance with a man's emotions for that to happen. Maturity is necessary to understand that saying certain statements and acting in certain ways only shows selfishness.

Men are also selfish at times. It is understandable that a man can't easily become "just friends" with someone from a previous relationship. Instead of being happy for a woman's newly-found happiness, some men hold a grudge. To purposely become an obstacle or dagger in the progress of the woman's new relationship is very immature. The "once mine, always mine" mentality is not only stupid, but can be dangerous too—mentally, emotionally, and physically. Too much time and energy gets poured into getting people to comfort our selfishness. We are neither being fair to them, nor to ourselves.

Something to Consider:

- _A square is always a rectangle by definition, but a rectangle has to meet certain requirements to be a square._

My favorite subject in school was mathematics. I remember learning that a rectangle is defined as a quadrilsteral (4-sided polygon) that consists of four right (90°) angles and whose opposite sides are parallel. A square is defined as a quadrilateral with four right angles <u>and</u> whose opposite sides are parallel <u>and</u> equal in length. So the above statement holds true. A square is always a rectangle, but a rectangle is not always a square.

With regards to the *Chase vs. Court* subject, *courting* is like the square, while *chasing* is like the rectangle. Chasing is more general, while courting is more specific. Courting each other in a relationship may include chasing somewhat, but to chase alone is only benefitting one person. Chasing will require more effort to fit the requirements of courting.

See, I knew all of those geometry assignments would come in handy!

Chapter 2

The Chase is too blurred

Communication, communication, communication

Some things are better left unsaid, and this principle is very important when knowing how to address a woman with a mature vocabulary. Men confuse having "game" with poor diction and women are not happy with the man's vocabulary when being pursued. I have always said that calling a woman by a name other than her given name is the quickest way to be dismissed from her memory. The pursuit ends before it really begins because of the man's decision to address a woman in the way he chooses versus what is appropriate to say. Here are some examples of what not to say:

 1. Calling a woman by her apparel:
 "Hey there blue shirt!"
 - makes her look superficial
 2. Calling a woman *"sexy"*:

- As much as she wants to feel sexy, you
don't know her well enough yet to address
her that way.
3. Calling a woman out of her name:
- When has profanity ever been attractive?
- Backlash can occur because she's offended.

On the other end of the spectrum, women can easily offend a man by the way she addresses him. Viewing him as an object and not a person can just as easily end a chase that may not have begun yet. Calling him "sexy" may not always be offensive to him as a man, but he deserves to be called by his given name just like a woman deserves it. Now, if we are to be honest, most men will find it appeasing to their ego if a woman actually addresses them as "sexy." Nevertheless, if a man isn't familiar with the woman saying it, then it can make him uncomfortable.

Sometimes, it is not the use of strong adjectives that makes a person turn in the opposite direction. Slang, in general, should have limitations on its usage when addressing someone of interest. We all have moments where something we say isn't grammatically correct, but overall we should strive to sound as intelligent as we look. Conversations should match our maturity levels, beginning with *how* we engage in those conversations. Otherwise, the chase reaches a dead end quickly.

Slang comes with familiarity as well, during moments where maturity isn't questioned anymore, and it is clear that a downtime moment of laughter, joking and/or relaxation exists. From a woman's standpoint, if a she is actually addressed by a man in the same manner to which he addresses his "homeboys," he is losing that pursuit because she cannot see where she is held in a more refined, much higher regard. If she feels that she is being addressed in the same manner as other females are addressed, then she definitely doesn't feel special and she will not remain interested in what that man says.

Still, there is a flip side to this scenario. Men like to know that when a certain lady is speaking with him, he is having a tailor-made conversation just for him. If he falls into the usual way a woman speaks with her male friends, a man will lose interest romantically. In his thinking, if what he says and how he says it doesn't draw the woman into admiration to hear more, or simply respond in a romantically-equivalent manner, he won't pursue any longer. There is nothing more he can do to separate him from the other male friends she knows because his conversation was one of his high points. If that conversation didn't gain any ground for him, then he is left to ponder what he can do next to gain interest from her. Often, the chase stops there.

Just be clear

Explaining the difference between "chase" and "court" opens up another topic that is so often overlooked in relationships. I have always valued clarity in any relationship – social, work-related, family, friendship, and so on. But clarity can only come from communication between everyone involved. Imagine a scenario where three friends are trying to plan an outing, and only two of them are in the loop of decision-making. Unless they know that third friend's wishes, thoughts, or opinions beforehand, making any final decisions without that person's input can not only ruin the outing itself, but can also ruin their friendship. Relationships between two people are no different.

Often in the early stages of the dating—what can be described as the "chasing" stage, communication is not as clear as it should be, yet, it is most necessary here. If a man is in an active pursuit of a lady, receives her contact information, they have a few conversations, and even arrange a date—the antenna needs to go up for the man (and woman) as to what that situation means, represents or could become. This doesn't mean that the two should immediately begin planning a wedding, but simply to keep their mind sharp enough to see what may or may not happen. Communication almost always dwindles as the dates begin to increase. If the woman is thinking that an exclusive situation is being formed, but the man is not, mixed emotions and even anger can arise. It can even be vice-versa for a man. The two sides may need clarity to understand a few principles, such as:

1. This is just a date—nothing else.
2. I like you, but I don't know you enough to feel anything otherwise.
3. I am not looking for anything serious.
4. This is not a green light to call me your girlfriend/boyfriend.
5. This is not a date. We're just "hanging out."

Statements like these can either make two people face the truth of the situation or run away from it altogether. Honesty isn't always harsh, but refusing to be straight-forward at all is a dangerous move. If the only box in which a particular guy fits is the "friend zone," then a woman should be courageous and truthful about it. If she wants a relationship, and he does not, then he needs to be vocal about it. He should not find more satisfaction in being quiet than in telling the truth. He shouldn't juggle the emotions she carries for him. Compassion and respect for feelings are important, but never should they be reason to not communicate about what is present.

So what are we?

This question is potentially an argument-starter and confusion-builder, but at least it starts the communication, if there wasn't any happening, or if there wasn't enough dialogue occurring. It is a question that has to be answered at some point. If two "intransitive" people (see previous chapter) date each other, this question is almost non-existent and off-the-table, because there is a clear understanding that those two individuals are just "going with the flow" of their situation. Whether they date long-term or not at all doesn't matter to them. Where this question becomes important is when one person feels that a "relationship" has started, yet, the other person feels it is more like "friendship." There are terms that we use in everyday communication that, when applied to dating situations, creates so much confusion. Many men will only pursue what is clear and they are justified in doing so.

One of the terms I absolutely hated when I would interact with a young lady was "talking." It was too vague, too general, and would often create an uncomfortable situation for me. I think a term like "talking" is one that doesn't appeal to logical thinking. The way I see it: we "talk" to people every day, we "talk" to people we randomly meet, and we even "talk" to people with whom we will never have a relationship. So why give that same term to someone I have been actually dating for weeks or months. If we only speak on the telephone, then we're "talking." But once those phone conversations spark time spent and interacting together, you're no longer just "talking."

Grown men have no problem being monogamous. Yet, if a woman tells him they're just "talking," she is inviting the admiration of another woman into her realm of attraction for that guy. If a man knows that the woman who has his attraction wants to give that attraction back to him exclusively, they will both consciously reject the word "talking." They each will have the understanding that they are (both collectively and individually) greater than that word, more valuable than that word, and are too logical for that word as a definition of the bond they now share.

If a woman wants a man to pursue her, she has to avoid the use of vague terms to define what she and her male counterpart are to each other. If he is just a friend, she should just say that. If he is the man she is exclusively dating, say that.

But she can almost guarantee confusion to exist if there is not a strong, definite answer when he asks: "Who I am to you?"

Other words such as, "seeing" "chilling with" "hanging out with" "kicking it with" all serve the same purpose of not defining the role of both parties in the dating situation. I'm not saying there should be pressure to rush and define something. If one is unsure, then so be it. But what should take place is the conversation explaining that unsure feelings exist. Women: Take your time to get know the man of interest, but don't expect him to not wonder about where he stands currently, and where he could go with you as well.

The Friend Zone

Men can get placed in the dreaded "Friend Zone" and will immediately view it as if it is a dungeon of no return. Many times, it becomes the permanent box for a man, even after he has shown great promise to exist at a much higher status for the woman. The disappointment of being in this box comes from a chase that turned into a dead end. Now, if we are honest, many of us men don't see the signs that warn us to make a turn off from the chase, or that the "Friend Zone" is coming up ahead of us. Then, once there, we're upset at the women. That's not fair to them. At the same time, all it takes is one time of chasing a woman and ending in the "Friend Zone" to make us not chase the next one.

Men who actually accept the Friend Zone for what it is usually find it too risky to pursue that same woman again. I have always had the philosophy that it is better to the be the friend she can stand, whose presence she accepts, or push to be something that she doesn't want from me, causing her to hate being around me. Some men feel that the Friend Zone is the minor league of dating or relationships. After a brief moment of time spent there, they feel they are ready for the major league pursuit. But that only makes a woman want to trade him for another "friend." (I'm a fan of sports, can't you tell?) Gambling a friendship to hopefully gain more than that can just as easily leave a man with neither the friendship nor dating relationship. The concept of "grass is greener on the other side" has easily left some men with no one.

Being in the Friend Zone can make a man a loyal, well-trusted, valuable friend to a woman if he accepts that position. The problem comes when his loyalty and value increases to the point where the woman sees him in a different light—one that increases her admiration and attraction towards him. But unless she turns the table and actually pursues him, he won't know his worth to her. If she placed him in that box, it is up to her to free him and/or promote him from that box. He isn't a mind-reader and furthermore, he won't "chase" her again most likely.

<u>*Something to Consider*</u>:

- *How uneasy are we at being called the wrong title in aspects of our lives (professional titles especially – Doctor, Professor, etc.)? Yet, when it comes to the pursuit of someone, we run from the same need to call (or be called) a title that is "proper"?*

In the academic world, people pursue high levels of education in order to advance in their professional goals. With each level of instruction, workloads seem more tedious, requiring more from the student—physically, mentally, emotionally, and of course, financially. But when all of the work is completed, nothing is greater than the sense of accomplishment that comes with obtaining the titles, initials, or other credentials the come with completing a particular program of study.

Students who complete doctoral programs (medical, educational, etc.) earned the right to be called "Doctor." Those who earned the title of "Professor," "Maestro," or "Reverend" also deserve the respect of being called those titles. So in love and romance, if a person has put forth the time, effort, sincerity, and affection to be called more than just your "friend," then say that. Discuss what title works for both sides, but be fair.

II.

THE "MENTAL" CHASE

Chapter 3

The Chase is too unfamiliar

Ladies: let's pretend that you are sitting in a chair at the beauty shop. Your regular hair stylist is not there. Suddenly, someone you don't know comes to cut and style your hair. Upon asking this new stylist how long she has been in the cosmetology field, she informs you that she isn't a hair stylist and that she has never taken a course in it. How comfortable will you be with her holding the scissors? She is clearly *unfamiliar* with the process of styling hair. She is also *unfamiliar* with you as a client—the hairstyles you like as well as the conversations shared between you and your regular stylist. So here comes the bigger question: If a novice will face difficulty trying to style your hair because of unfamiliarity, how can a man, who is also unfamiliar with you, effectively "chase" after you?

Women have to understand that not every man has been taught the subject of courting. Instead of expecting him to approach with the utmost confidence, understand there may be some hindrances in the way. He wants to speak, he wants to be courteous, he wants to be smooth, but he may lack some attributes to do so. The way society defines chivalry, or having "game" and "swagger," affects a man's ability to pursue a woman of interest.

Does he have "game"?

The word *game* can be defined using many adjectives that enable a man to approach a woman (and vice-versa). As much as words like *confidence, charisma, intelligence,* or even *chivalry* describe a man's "game" in a positive way, words like *arrogant, cocky, self-absorbed* can easily give a negative tone to it. Nevertheless, *game* has become a ticket to how men earn the woman's attention, how he cleverly draws her interest into who he is (or who he wants her to think he is), and how smooth he looks doing so. There seems to be a buffet table of elements that any one man can use to say he has game – everything from simple compliments to complex strategy and methods to show a woman he is seriously trying to win her affection.

Chivalry isn't dead, but for some, it was never born.

Chivalry is an old knighthood term describing the attributes necessary for someone who wanted to be a noble knight. These ideal qualities include loyalty, confidence, courtesy, honor, and generosity. No man is born automatically with these qualities. They are learned over time.

Parents, other immediate and extended family members, friends, and mentors all serve as influential vessels to not only talk about chivalry, but to display it. In households where male figures are deemed not important or are simply non-existent, the passing-down of chivalry falls to the female. She has to teach her young son, young nephew, or young cousin how to pull out a lady's chair for her to sit, open doors for her, or pick up something of hers that may have been dropped on the floor. Some things are difficult for a female to teach a young male, but if she doesn't, it is possible no one else will.

A man may have a great education, a sense of humor, and a great career, but lack the chivalry necessary to appropriately approach and pursue a woman. A man can get caught up with society's definition of "game" and feel that if he approaches a woman in his own way, he will be successful. Depending on the woman approached, that mindset will not work. Chivalry isn't negating the idea of being creative in one's approach, but if the creativity is too extreme, it will be difficult to see sincerity behind the man's action.

Missing the signs

I don't recall any moments where I just felt like I had enough "game" to charm a young lady. I wasn't good at jokes, or pickup lines, and I never thought I could win with just a "hello" and a smile. (Now, my smile was very important to me, especially once I had braces because they made my smile better. Why not show it more?) Yet, there were times when I completely underestimated myself. There were a few instances that I would be called a "flirt," but in my mind, I was simply having a nice conversation, or giving a compliment, which was normal to me because I was raised by my parents and grandmother to be a gentleman. I didn't think that it made me any more attractive than if I remained silent.

My high school/college friends would laugh at me because I was clueless when a girl or young lady supposedly flirted with me. Perhaps, in her mind, she wasn't good enough for me to reciprocate the flirtation, but I was just unaware that the situation called for that. Don't get me wrong, I wasn't socially inept, in my opinion, but because of nervousness, or even my own self-perception, flirtation was a subject I hadn't conquered at that time. Some men are just unfamiliar with pursuing a woman sometimes because we just miss the signs.

Signals crossed

It's funny enough that as a poet, I have written many poems about love, relationships, friendships, etc. that would give a reader the impression that I have so much "game" to "woo" women with words. Sure, my words may stir thoughts and opinions, but never have they served as "game." I think I just spoke my mind and heart in an art form. But I do understand how that can come off differently to other people.

Not only can the "chase" serve to be unfamiliar to the man, but also to the woman. His unfamiliarity may affect hers. Because of poor definition, lack of instances where chasing occurred, or perhaps, the attitude of entitlement to be chased, women can easily become disappointed. It is because they are unfamiliar with how their men of interest operate. If a woman is not familiar with chivalry from men she has previously encountered, she may not know how to handle a man offering a compliment, smiling at her while he says "good morning," one giving up his seat for her, or offering to carry her bags.

She may prematurely and incorrectly assume those gestures are apart the man's "game," but he is actually just being nice. If she responds harshly to those gestures, it sends a message to him that she is not worth chasing at all. She may also be unaware of anyone else who witnessed her response. If other men saw that, they won't pursue either.

Something to Consider

In baseball, teams use hand signs to communicate on aspects like pitching, hitting, bunting, and also stealing bases. Although they look confusing to viewers, hand signs act as a code language for teams to instruct players, but also to confuse the opposing teams. But when a player goes to another team, some of the same sign gestures mean different things. If that newest player tries to use old signs, or interprets the signs for something his old team did, the current team can lose the game. Team chemistry can be disrupted as well.

Communicate any changes of signals when pursuing or dating someone new. The new person of interest may not know how your flirtation looks or feels. Confusion may make innocent miscommunication seem like a deliberate action of not caring. An assumption of what one means or feels can lead to disappointment when actions are expected, but not executed.

Chapter 4

The Chase is too familiar

Sometimes, what a man doesn't know may prevent a chase. But at other times, what he knows too well ends the chase for him. When people take a hard look at themselves first, then look at others around them, sometimes painful truths are revealed. Relationships and friendships can possibly end because of too much familiarity. Fear, misunderstanding, and anger can arise out of revealing what some may not want to hear. Although situations may be new, they may show signs of previous situations that didn't turn out so well. They may also provide the likelihood of hurt and disappointment, or prompt the intuition to leave and run away.

Point of No Return

Friendship is a very important bond that is shared between two or more people. To know that there is another person who appreciates your intelligence, dependability, strength, laughter, etc., is a wonderful feeling to have.

Because of its value, friendship is also taken for granted sometimes, and used as a reason to pursue something deeper. But unless it is somehow protected by both sides and there is a mutual understanding of the value it really has, friendships become the "point of no return" when pursuing relationships. As a result, if the relationship somehow doesn't last (even if it is mutual and not because of any wrongdoing), the man and woman can't go back to being friends so easily. Furthermore, this relationship becomes a point of familiarity for both sides when pursuing or being pursued by the next person.

A man has female friends, just as a woman has male friends. What keeps those friendships in their respective lanes is the understanding that the friendship has more value in its current state than at any other time of its existence. It will not have more value after the relationship ends, and sometimes friendships unknowingly die to the relationship. Friendships outside of the relationships die too at times. Now, let me be clear: some outside friendships need to end if they are deemed detrimental to any two people's relationship. But regardless of how much a man adores a woman, he won't chase her if he feels or see signs that it will end just like a previous friendship-turned-relationship ended. Some men just won't take the risk.

Reputation speaks volumes

Another aspect of familiarity to consider is the reputation of a person. We live in a world now where everyone knows everyone else—via mutual friendships and/or mutual acquaintances, newly-discovered family connection, and/or social media connections. It is not that difficult for a person's private life to become public in a short span of time. As much as this may hurt one's goal to stay hidden out of everyone else's view, knowing the reputation of someone can also prove to be beneficial.

Knowing a man's reputation allows women to avoid pitfalls of immaturity, infidelity, and ignorance. Just the same, knowing the woman's reputation is just as much a reason not to chase as it is a good one to pursue. Not everything a man finds out about a woman is negative, but if it is the truth, it saves the man from disappointment and heartache nonetheless. It allows the man to recall instances of familiarity similar to the current situation that somehow didn't end too well.

For instance, if a man discovers that the woman of his interest does not like to watch sports, yet he is the biggest fan of sports, he knows the chances of taking that woman to his favorite games are very slim. He may tell himself that she is not worth it because of what he knows ahead of time. If she doesn't like children, but he is always around his niece and nephew, then he can determine right away that maybe he shouldn't pursue. He knows her before any confusion arises. Again, a man will not pursue what shows the strong possibility of not working.

<u>Something to Consider:</u>

- *Can a friendship be restored once the attempt to have a romantic relationship fails? If so, how does that journey back to friendship begin?*
- *If reputation speaks volumes, why is it sometimes "muted" for the sake of affection? Is muting the reputation viewed more as a sacrifice for the relationship or is it viewed as stupidity?*

We addressed friendship-turned-relationship situations as a "point of no return." But for some people, there exists the need to restore a friendship that was deemed lost. There is no set roadmap back to friendship. The only thing that can repair or restore a broken friendship is *time*. If the person(s) who ruined the friendship cannot show presence and compassion towards the heartbroken, damaged friend, then the friendship will never be repaired. Both sides must be prepared to have open and honest dialogue. For some, the hurt is too severe to address, and those feelings must be respected. Let your actions be a reflection of the lessons learned from the torn friendships, and hope that your former friends see that. If it is meant for that friendship to exist, it will exist again. But if it's meant to be a learning point and holds the purpose for maturity and growth, then so be it. You can't force love, even on a friendship level.

Sometimes, we tend to "mute" what we know because what we know isn't convenient, or comfortable. When we know someone has a bad reputation, we shouldn't condemn them, but there should be a light bulb that comes on in our minds saying, "I don't need to be bad with them." You can show support, encourage, give hope, teach and instruct, and above all, pray for the person's reputation to change for the better. But, never should you think that you carry the absolute ability to change them because you are with them in a romantic relationship.

Sometimes, we think that we are making a sacrifice for a relationship when we dim the light on certain aspects of a person. Women sacrifice their standards because they feel they can't find the right man. Men sacrifice being chivalrous and respectful because they have been told at some point that women like it when men "tell them what to do." That's not sacrifice, that's stupidity. Sacrifice is not about refusing to compromise, but simply about complementing the other person. But it is stupid to ignore the fact that someone's reputation just doesn't fit with yours. You can ignore the fact that your love interest wastes money, but you will be broke, too, in the end. You can ignore the fact that your love interest calls you out of your name, but then you will begin calling yourself out of your name. That's not a sacrifice for love, but rather, that's settling for stupidity in order to keep love.

Chapter 5

The Chase is too intimidating

Strengths vs. Weaknesses

Everyone has strengths—regardless as to whether or not they are easily seen. On the other hand, where there are strengths, there are also weaknesses. A complementary relationship exists between the two sides. When a man (excuse me, a mature man) sees a woman that interests him, he soon looks past the exterior beauty and seek to discover her strengths. He is not looking at her strengths just to make a tally sheet of her greatness, but rather, to see what strengths she has that may match his weaknesses.

If a man is mature enough, he will have very little difficulty exposing some of his weaknesses to a woman. I'm not talking about spilling out every little flaw he may have, but if he simply acknowledges where she is better than he is at certain things, a long-lasting bond can form. The same goes for women opening up too. The problem is that the greatness of a woman is viewed differently by men than it is by other women. The greatness of a man is seen differently by women as well.

Both sides need to understand that a complement system only strengthens what they have together as well as what they have individually. People need to stop trying to compete and match each other to the utmost degree. We are not equal at everything. The "50-50" mentality, for some, may need to be replaced by the "50% average" mentality. In other words, by recognizing the strengths and weaknesses of each other, it may be concluded that when it comes to money, it's 80-20 percent in favor or the woman, but when it comes to communication, it is 70-30 percent in favor of the man. When you add 80 and 20 together, or add 70-30 together, they respectively both equal 100 (as in 100 percent). When that 100% is divided by 2 (meaning the man and woman involved), that is now 50%. Each person will represent 50% without having to defend their equality to each other.

If men felt that their weaknesses were being viewed as stepping stones or the cohesive steps to a woman's strengths, then the pursuit will forever be a thrill to him. He will be able to trust her with his emotions, because he won't be viewed as "weak" but as "strong-in-progress." Always seek to find the positive outlet to his affection, not the negative outlet to his weaknesses, and he'll never run away and hide.

Her light shines brighter

Since the beginning of time, the man has always been viewed as the leader, protector, overseer, the one who directs the path for his family to follow. God made man the leader of the household, but not to diminish the character of a woman. The woman has an important role as the nurturer, the giver, the preparer, the one who makes the home comfortable. She is the perfect complement to the man. Men and women are not meant to be exclusively independent of each other, but to coexist interdependently. They are to aid each other, care for each other, and build a foundation together. That attitude and viewpoint is really absent from today's society.

Because of other circumstances, the roles of a woman have to be altered in some instances. The woman who is faced with the situation of raising her children alone because the father isn't there (for whatever reason—no judgment) has to be the protector and nurturer, the leader and the second-in-command, the overseer and the one who executes. She is both mother and father-like. So as her children see her do it all as though she has super powers, she shapes an image in their minds. What that does for a son: it gives him the template of the woman he needs to find when he is an adult. But what that does for a daughter: it shows her just how much a woman can do without the aid of a man.

Because so many young men grow up without a male figure present, their perception of manhood is sometimes missing something. It's like a recipe that needs just a pinch more spice to be great. If that man becomes attracted to a woman who is like the one just mentioned, he may come face-to-face with insecurities that he may or may not have been aware of before then. These insecurities can be passed down to future sons and grandsons, and while no fault all their own, they can easily be viewed by a woman as weaknesses. Sometimes, this happens even if there were male role models present for a boy during his growing years.

Worthiness despite insecurity

There are several reasons why a man can feel insecure in his life. As a child or young teen, males face the issue of bullying, body changes, voice changes, social interaction, popularity and more—all of which can affect how he sees himself. This self-analysis continues into adulthood and never goes away for some men. Despite achieving great things in his own life, a man can still feel insecure. I can recall several instances where my own insecurity prevented me from achieving my dreams at the time.

I started wearing glasses at age 9, and as grateful as I was that my vision was better, I didn't care much for the names that came with needing those glasses. Names like "nerd," "geek," "four-eyes" etc., made me feel that I wasn't handsome. I was (and still am currently) very skinny, so adding poor vision to that was not ideal. My self-esteem wasn't great at all, so when I became interested in a certain girl, I was always too afraid to speak. With each level of schooling, from elementary, to middle and high schools, I was never 100 percent comfortable with my appearance, not even with contact lenses. I had to change how I viewed myself, which took time, but also took the understanding that I'm worthy of anything to which I set my mind, even I was slightly insecure.

It wasn't just my vision that caused problems, but also it was my voice. As a young adult, I never liked how my voice sounded to anyone else. One day, I overheard a voicemail from a friend of mine. I jokingly asked: "Who is that on your message?" I said that as if the voice was weird or funny, but when I realized that it was me, I was dumbfounded. I couldn't believe I sounded like that on a voicemail message. As much as I liked performing poetry at open-mic nights, I would have to continuously tell myself to get over my fears and insecurities in order to perform without any issues.

A woman may feel that a guy fits the mold of everything she is looking for relationship-wise, but if he is insecure, he may not pick up the clues she may send in his direction. His physical appearance, the way his voice sounds on a telephone call, or the way he walks—may each have favor from the woman's standpoint, but may be the reasons why the man doesn't pursue. He doesn't feel great about himself. There were a few girls who probably liked me back as a teen/young adult, but because I was insecure, I didn't realize it, and often didn't act on their signals—a smile or wave of hello.

Another aspect to consider: some men are very observant. If he notices the groups of people a woman usually entertains with her time, he may not ever approach if he feels inferior. If a man has a career picking up garbage (nothing wrong with that at all—let's be clear), but notices the woman he admires only associates with doctors, lawyers, engineers, and entrepreneurs, then he may feel "less than" and not worthy enough to pursue her. It isn't her fault for being great in her career and in her social arena, but it doesn't lessen his viewpoint either. Some may say that he isn't insecure, but just observant. A woman who looks at a man as if her status makes her "better" than him, will also cause him to stop his pursuit before it even begins. It is up to her to even the playing field. He will pursue if he feels he has a strong case in his favor. But if his intuition says that the game is over before it begins, he simply won't begin.

Something to Consider:

- *Ladies: were you aware that you can intimidate men? Do you know of (or can you recall) moments where you individually intimidated a man?*
- *Looking back, can you see where you unknowingly or unintentionally intimidated a man? Do you think that man was interested in you romantically?*
- *How difficult is it to hear that women are intimidating?*
- *How difficult is it for a man to admit to a woman that she is intimidating? Is it worth mentioning versus walking away entirely?*
- *How can a woman's income level affect a man's intimidated mindset? In what ways can she help him resolve his issues despite making more money than him?*

Rather than turn these questions into another chapter altogether, they are strictly meant for ladies to use in discussion, or in self-evaluation. They are not meant to point the finger at women, in general, but to show that this chapter can easily flow off the page into daily life. Ladies, feel free to ask the men in your lives to chime in on the answers.

They may have been afraid or cautious to tell you that you are intimidating. But communicate with love at heart, so that you don't disrespect each other, but that the honesty of these questions make you respect each other more.

III.

THE "PHYSICAL" CHASE

Chapter 6

The Chase is too unrealistic

Ask any man, and it is almost a guarantee that, at some point, he was told that his memory is not good or that he doesn't pay attention to what a woman says. Although it is true for some, there is another aspect that is not always understood. Men pay close attention to what a woman says, but there is a point where he tunes her out, or detours his mind away from the conversation. The point where this occurs is what I call the "point of non-reality." If the words coming out of her mouth are so unrealistic that he cannot understand it, perceive it, fulfill it, or accept it, he will no longer be engaged in that conversation. Realistically, he is simply not the kind of man who will show interest to what doesn't make sense.

What kind of man are you looking for?

People make lists for everything—grocery lists, gift lists, to-do lists, and so on. So, it's not foreign to think that when a lady is asked about attributes that her potential date, boyfriend, or husband should have, there's a list for that too. There is not a problem with that process, but sometimes what lands on that list may prompt a huge STOP sign to a man who wants to pursue her. Even in relationships and marriages, the continuous pursuit of that special lady may have a kink in it now because of that list. Some attributes are necessary and should be on any woman's list. These qualities may include: being educated, sharing the same faith, having goals, and having manners. No one will have problems with those qualities being listed. But when qualities become too superficial or shallow, it makes the man look away, turn away, and run away. No man wants to know that your list is so specific that he has no room for growth. Better yet, he doesn't want to feel that he was never satisfactory in the first place.

Evaluating the List

Imagine a man's thoughts if a woman says something like this:

> "I want a man who is at least 6'3" with no children. He has to live in a large home and drive a top-of-the line car or SUV. He has to make a six-figure salary, and have a big bank account. He has to have pretty eyes and a physique that shows how much he works out at the gym. He should have a great wardrobe of name-brand clothing and shoes. His hair has to be cut short, he has to have a full-beard and he should have at least 3 tattoos. He has to love to travel also."

Now let's be clear: there is nothing wrong with wanting the attributes on this list. A woman has every right to want these qualities in a man, whether he likes it or not. The problem with a list like this is the fact that the attributes are all assembled on the same list. Individually, each attribute has its own value associated with it. For example, if a woman is 6'2" tall, then it's understandable why she may prefer a man who is 6'3" in his height. She may want to stare into his "pretty" eyes. That doesn't sound unreasonable. But when a woman compiles every single attribute she desires in man within the same list, she opens herself for criticism and potentially disappointment.

What are the chances of her finding the man with <u>every</u> quality on her list? What are the chances he meets half of them? There is nothing wrong with being selective, and there is certainly nothing wrong with being patient. But if a woman has a list of unrealistic attributes that she wants in a man, she may encounter just the opposite. Some men are willing to fake or flourish the attributes a woman prefers because he knows that he will never meet them. From the man's standpoint, he is chasing perfection in order to be with her, and that's not healthy for either of the two sides.

The Upside

Instead of making a list of unrealistic characteristics of her ideal man, maybe it is more beneficial for a woman to pick the three most important ones and start there. As men, we aren't stupid. If we know we bring a strong sense of accomplishment, attitude, and compassion, and those qualities don't meet a woman's standards, then we will no longer pursue. A man knows he doesn't stand a chance to be with a woman who wants more than any one man can give. Often, good men are overlooked because they aren't ideal. But by closing the door on his personal characteristics, a woman is also closing the door on his future upward climb.

Some attributes are subject to change and some are going to remain in the arena they're in currently. Things like height (for adults) and eye color won't change, while the materialistic objects—house, car, money, etc. can come and go. Hobbies and personal likes/dislikes can change as well. The point is to carefully evaluate what a man has going in the direction you favor before you totally dismiss him. Try to see potential in the areas you like that he possibly hasn't "perfected" yet. For instance, if he meets your physical likes (height, weight, hair, eye color, etc.) as well as your mental likes (well-educated, well-spoken), but has yet to make the six-figure salary, try to see the *upside* to his development.

Does he have the potential to make a higher salary, not for you, but for himself? Does he value your opinion of him enough to realize that he can achieve more, and that you can help him do so? Sometimes, when a man knows you value what he already brings to the table, he will work harder to bring more, or simply bring a bigger table. He's not "chasing" after you, but more after the life you influence him to have.

But there is a catch: a woman must pay attention to two aspects within herself. First, she must realize when she being contradictory. A woman says she wants a man with a nice bank account. Okay, that is fine. But to immediately say that he must have the latest and greatest clothes, shoes, car, house, etc. only negates having a nice bank account for most men. He may choose to focus his riches on items that won't lose value, or may benefit his future, not his present. If his bank account is enough for him to do have those things, adding her and her wants to the equation will quickly diminish that bank account. He really may need to make six figures! Some things are so ideal, that it is easy to overlook the fact that they cannot exist with other ideal things. For every ideal object or situation, there needs to be a dose of reality that disputes aspects of that situation.

Secondly, a woman must understand when she is also placed under her own microscope. As much as her preferences are verbalized and displayed, there are moments where she doesn't realize that she is incapable of receiving what she is asking for. If she says she wants a man with a great education, he is going wonder what school she attended. If she says she wants a man with a nice bank account, he is going to wonder what debts she has. He is going to measure her using the same lens she uses on him to look into his current situation. In fact, he may use a lens with deeper magnification to show her parts of herself she may not have known to exist.

The question for women to consider is this: Who is he really chasing—the "you" that looks good in the future, or the one that doesn't look so good now? A man who knows the quality he possesses will not chase after a woman who places all of her hopes on wishes for her future, if all he sees is the downfall of her present state and mindset. If he is more attracted to the woman's future, her dreams, her passions more than she is, the "chase" will end rather quickly—that is, if it begins at all.

We Are What We Watch

Over the last decade, television has transitioned from the comedies, action, and drama that many people watched from childhood through adolescence and adulthood. Television shows were once the forum where writers actually wrote solid scripts with real plots, subplots, and interesting characters, and had quality actors to act out the scenes. Nowadays, "reality TV" has become the forefront of what television viewing means, bringing redundancy in its format—constant arguing, fighting, cursing, backstabbing, deceit, conceit, and more, all in the name of "entertainment."

I have always carried a certain philosophy about "entertainment" that seems correct in many cases. My philosophy is that we are what we watch on television. For instance, in most cases, if a person watches basketball all of the time, rarely missing a game, he/she is really an athlete at the core. That person may not possess the God-given ability to jump, shoot, pass, and run at the level of the professionals, but would probably trade places with them professionally without hesitation. (I'm referring to on-the-court only. Off-the-court lives are another subject.) Ask anyone who watches the food channels, crime/detective shows, or even shows about travel. I believe there are many who would feel that we have a piece of the characters, hosts, and stars within us. That is what keeps us intrigued.

So, how is it any different when it comes to some of these raunchy reality shows? It isn't different at all. I know that it isn't just women who watch them, but men as well. There are a few reasons why reality shows are a bad influence for both men and women romantically:

> 1. They give men the notion that they should have a woman that will tolerate their stupidity, immaturity, and disrespect all in the name of loyalty. This only decreases the value of the women who attract (and are attracted to) these men.

> 2. The TV shows provide a ridiculous platform that allows women to fight other women over a man who completely disrespects both of them. Women cursing and slapping other women is never an attractive aspect to mature men. Why should a man chase either one of them?

> 3. It gives women the sense of entitlement that they deserve the fashion, purses, the best hair weaves, the jewelry, the houses, cars, etc., when it isn't guaranteed that those "characters" actually own those things. Start with your own money, because no man is going to chase after "broke."

When all is said and done, it is terrible to think that women actually "want" to be these people seen on reality television shows. Women are better off watching love movies that show them how they should be treated, because reality shows are only showing them who not to become.

Just be real

There is nothing more immature than being phony. It boggles my mind to think that people would much rather put on layers of fabrication rather than be honest with themselves. It is an insult to someone's common sense to be phony, not just because being phony is wrong in itself, but also from the fact that even without demonstration, the phony nature was already discovered before anything was said. Actions are indeed louder than words, and cities are looking smaller and smaller. What we think no one knows is actually known by many.

There is no need for a man to pretend he is, he has, or he once was something that is false. We live in a society where so many things are traceable. The technology is there to find information about a person to help verify what he or she said or did. Mutual friends or associates often serve as the link between verifying the truth and uncovering a lie. If a man says he works for a certain business firm, his status can be checked immediately nowadays. Word-of-mouth is still a powerful tool for finding information. Usually, it is not too difficult to use other known sources to inquire about someone.

We must also be mature in regards to material things in our lives. Those things that we present to our "fans" show only what we want them to see. Individuals who are closer to us know the truth. Today's world seems centered around who-has-what, and how much of it exists. A man can be enormously rich, but be mentally and emotionally immature. So ladies, the next time a man starts to mention what he does, how much he has, what he owns, who he knows, etc., verify that. This will prevent you from being chased by the wrong man, in the wrong race. Men, when a woman does the same thing, verify that as well. This way, your time will not be wasted running a race that could very well lead you nowhere.

<u>Something to Consider:</u>

- *Why is a man's "upside" ignored by some women? Why must the "total package" be the only option?*
- *Take your favorite reality shows to watch on television. Now ask yourself: how do these shows impact my mindset about romantic relationships? Are you more likely or less likely to get the person you want based off the influence given by these shows?*
- *A man should be real, but there should be a balance of being real, and not using "realness" as an excuse for being less. Being real exhibits the truth, but is not a restriction for attempting to be a better person in every aspect of life.*

This is where I hope that just as many men are reading this book as women are. The men may have some valid answers to why they are ignored by women. Women have come in contact with various types of men and feel that they don't have time to wait for a man's "upside" to flourish. They much rather have a man at his "apex" or his highest point—financially, academically, emotionally, etc. But one thing to consider: after the apex is reached, there is usually a downward descent. By changing the perception, the results change too. Always view his "upside" as just that—a constant uphill climb to his most successful self. It shows the need to consistently strive for greater, while still appreciating and being grateful for the current position. It diminishes arrogance, because a man will know that he is not finished, but rather, he still has plenty of "gas in the tank."

As for the reality shows, that question is perhaps one of the most honest questions to ask oneself. If we are honest, we will see the influence right away. But even if we don't see it immediately, the effect will show itself eventually. I really believe that.

Chapter 7

The Chase is too superficial

When the word *superficial* is usually said, it refers to a person being so shallow in the way he or she thinks. There is no depth to that person's logical mindset. The overall definition of *superficial* simply refers to things on the surface of something. With this definition, what is affects a man's chase is the outward appearance of the woman. In fact, it's the first thing that affects his interest in her. There is nothing wrong at all with a woman wanting to look her best. A woman's confidence and self-esteem is closely associated with how she sees herself. It makes plenty of sense for her to want to look attractive, stunning, gorgeous, and so on.

Is that really you?

Where the physical appearance takes on a more superficial perspective is when it diminishes, disguises, or detracts from what is naturally there. In today's modern

61

world, many products exist that serve the sole purpose of "enhancing" a woman's beauty. Everything from hair extensions, eyelash extensions, artificial nails, breast implants, pharmaceutical injections of various substances, and of course, facial makeup—exist to satisfy the woman's need to look her absolute best. But too much of a good thing is still too much.

Some enhancements are understandable more than others. For example, a woman loses one or both breasts to breast cancer and decides to undergo a complete makeover. For her, it's about retrieving a piece of her that was taken away by a disease. This helps in the healing process because she has a better sense of self, and as a survivor, she deserves the feeling of strength alongside a renewed sense of beauty. No decent man would argue that.

Problems arise when a woman's appearance becomes so hidden that a man is almost chasing a costumed version of her. Many men are not against the use of weaves or hair extensions. But there was once a time when men couldn't tell the difference between a woman's real hair and the added hair piece(s). Nowadays, because of its popularity, men are more familiar with the overall appearance of it. Odds are that he has dated at least one person who has worn weaves, wigs, braids, etc.

Some women will argue that unless they have been exclusively dating someone for an extended period of time, that particular man will not ever see her "cosmetically naked," meaning no makeup, no weave extensions, no artificial eyebrows, and so on. But that is not always the best decision.

A man will always want what he finds to be most familiar and makes him comfortable. If he meets a woman that is always in the full armor of the hair and makeup, it will be difficult to decrease that appearance because that is the impression he was left with by her. Then if he becomes un-attracted to her physically, he is labeled to be shallow, when it is really the woman who sparked his interest in how she looks.

Again, because some men have become more aware of the things women use to enhance themselves, some have become less intrigued. Instead, they (more often) want to see the woman without makeup, with her own hair (regardless of if it is natural or relaxed), without any forehead or lip injections, without any implants, etc. They want to know what the bottom level is with that woman. I call this the least common denominator.

In mathematics, the least common denominator was the lowest number that two fractions share in common. Men and women must come to that point where they see the truest version of each other. Some women are not going to go that far, but yet, they want the men to chase after them. But what are they chasing? A man "feeds" off what he sees first, and if a woman alters what he is used to seeing, she diminishes his appetite to "eat" off your "plate." You are then "serving" him food he isn't familiar with, or for which he hasn't "acquired a taste."

<u>Something to Consider:</u>

There are times

when he is not looking

for gorgeous, sexy, fine, or cute.

He is simply looking for YOU,

and the discovery of "beautiful"

in that person.

Chapter 8

The Chase is too exhausting

Racing and Pacing

Anyone who is familiar with running (track and field, cross-country, morning exercise, etc.) knows there are sprinters and long-distance runners. They have different styles and/or different approaches to their respective distances. Interestingly, if examined closely, the attributes associated with these two running types can also give insight to the approaches men and women face when discussing dating or relationships. The question people must ask themselves is: *"What kind of runner am I?"*

Sprinters are known for their speed. They know the distance that lies ahead of them and carry the realization that it will not take them long to reach that distance. To them, the whole objective is to race to the finish line. When referring to love/relationships, the goal is not necessarily to get there as fast as possible. It is more about not wasting time, energy, and steps. If a person can go from his/her home to work in 30 minutes, why take 45 minutes? The extra time and energy is unnecessary. For some men and women, it doesn't take long to know if someone is a romantic match, or will be compatible to one's reality. As much as individuals like these can fall in love quickly, they also can fall out of it just as fast.

Long-distance runners are those that embrace and enjoy the pace of their journey. They know that distance in advance just as sprinters do, but they have a better realization that the finish line is not going anywhere. They don't want to waste time and energy here either, and they are not going to over-extend themselves if the situation doesn't call for them to do so. Still, in the midst of their running, they run at a pace that shows comfort. They also have more endurance than most sprinters. So what does all of this information mean for men with regard to "chasing" or pursuing a woman? One word: *adaptation.*

Finding the Middle Distance

I can recall, back in high school, training for an upcoming track-and-field season. To get in shape, I ran one afternoon with a couple of long-distance runners. I was a sprinter (with half-decent speed) and never ran anything over 400 meters (or one lap) in any one track event. I would only run 800-1600 meters for conditioning, but not for time sake. The long-distance runners, on the other hand, were also cross-country runners who also ran the long-distance events for track. As much as I appreciated the jog, I couldn't keep up with them, and after running some of the distance near and around the campus, they had to leave me behind. I eventually finished the jogging, but I was winded. Looking in retrospect, it is easy to see now how the "chase" process has similarity to running.

Ideally, a sprinter would work well with other sprinters, and just the same, a long-distance runner with other long-distance runners. They are equal. A woman who sprints will have the pleasure of a man chasing her, because chances are he may run very closely. The beauty here is not just in the "chase," but also in the "race" itself. The male sprinter will accept the challenge of the chase, because he knows that after a short distance, the chase and the race ends, and they'll both reach the finish line within moments of each other or at the same time. They genuinely will enjoy each other's running style.

Two long-distance runners are just as equal and will also find beauty in the pace of the race and not just the chase. They will enjoy the journey of their race without feeling rushed to reach their finish line. They know it is some distance away from where they are presently. The idea of a chase is less important in this scenario because speed is not important, but finishing strong and together is their focus.

If a sprinter is chasing after a long-distance runner, he'll catch up to her, but once he does, he is ready to stop running. Even if he is not out of breath, he feels that his short distance was all that it took to catch up with his woman of interest. She is not ready to stop running so she continues until her long distance run ends at some point later. She is not impressed with speed, but with longevity.

If a long-distance runner is chasing after a sprinter, he will soon find himself running on a track by himself. She will quickly pass him by, but since he is a long-distance runner, he will not see the need to increase his speed solely because she is running past him. He may feel because he isn't running that fast, she'll take notice of his running while she is at rest. She may take his comfortable pace as just as an attempt to be seen or catch her eye.

The last two scenarios can work only if the two different sides agree to *adapt*. This brings to mind what is sometimes referred to as a middle-distance runner. In track and field, where your sprinters are typically your 100- and 200- meter sprinters, and long-distance runners are 1600- and 3200- meter racers, middle-distance runners are the 400-800 meter runners. These special runners are important because they great at adapting to the course.

Middle-distance runners are the perfect blend between speed and endurance. They may need to have a sprinter mindset at some point, but then also think long-distance at times. A sprinter can adapt to being a middle-distance runner by working on endurance and pacing steps correctly. A long-distance runner can work on speed to be more like a sprinter. The balance created here allows for both running types to have a healthy bond without one side feeling like the "chase" is required.

Run fast,

run slow,

but run only when your finish line

is in focus.

Chapter 9

The Chase is too uncertain

Depth Perception

Standard running tracks are 400 meters around in distance, so a person who has completed one lap has completed 400 meters. There are two curved portions as well as two straightway portions, each being 100 meters apiece. When standing at the start of a relay race, the first curve is ran initially. That first runner passes the baton to the second runner who runs the first straightway. The third runner gets the baton from the second to run the second curve, and finally the fourth runner runs the last straightway portion. Although there distances are equal, sometimes the perception or the view from the start of the curve is different from that when standing at the beginning of the straightway.

Standing at the start of a curve portion, it is easy to see a true sense of the 100 meter distance because you can see the entire curve from that position. In other words, the 100 meters actually looks like 100 meters. Standing from the starting point on the straightway portions, runners don't really get an accurate view of the 100 meters. They just know that it's at the end of that straight line they're going to run.

Depth perception refers the eye's ability to see the distances between things. In the pursuit of love and romance, it is difficult sometimes to see how much distance exist between two individuals. It is also hard sometimes to visualize the finish line. For some men, chasing after a woman looks like the straightway. If his chase is a 100-meter dash, he may think to himself that such a short distance shouldn't be difficult. He may take off running and gain much speed, but because of his poor depth perception, he may realize the finish line is not as close as he first thought. As a result, he is no longer enjoying the chase itself, and is unknowingly slowing down, because he is purposely searching for that finish line.

Some men may feel that getting a woman's attention, gaining her interest, obtaining her number or even dating her is not a hard challenge. That's because they are in the starting blocks of that chase. But once he realizes his charm isn't working, she isn't as interested, or conversation is not making her smile, laugh, or remain attentive, he realizes his race is not going as well as he hoped. That finish line that once looked so attainable now looks so far away, and the desire to finish the race, or "chase" is no longer there.

- _Another way to look at depth perception: Rather than give up, or lose momentum while running, a man will (or should) find a woman who will allow them both to shorten the length of the race. That ties back to courting vs. chasing all over again. If the race is shortened, you may effectively run 60 meters instead of 100 meters. The new finish line goal is reachable because you can see it better. This will also make both sides less afraid to race again over other hurdles once the relationship starts. A man will appreciate the woman who makes his race lighter and his vision better._

Chapter 10

The Chase has too many runners

Other runners in the race

Sometimes, men are not eager to pursue when they know odds are that they won't succeed. But what is worse to consider is the distraction of that chase. When runners line up on a track to complete a race, each one is competing for the same end result: to be first place. It is no different with pursuing a person. For some men competition is welcomed, understood to exist, and serves as no problem or threat. But for others, unless there is some incentive for entering the race in the first place, they feel no need to compete. It isn't about them being "too good" or above the nature of competing, but rather they just know their limitations.

If a man is pursuing a woman, both sides must not make the pursuit about the challenge itself. If a woman knows two men are pursuing her, she must deal with each one separately. Otherwise, what can occur is a situation where the two men are no longer concerned about her as the reward or first place, but rather, they are simply trying to out-perform each other. Competition becomes more about their "machismo" and "swagger" and less about the woman involved. It cheapens her value, and makes them look stupid.

Racing the Ex

Under no circumstances will a man pursue a woman if he knows that the ex-boyfriend, ex-husband, ex-whatever-title-used is still in the race. Think about the 8 runners in the track race. If it is known that one of the runners is an "ex" of some kind, it sends messages to the other runners. For instance, the new man who is pursuing the woman notices the ex-boyfriend is still present. The following questions are popping into his head immediately (or at least they should be there):

1. *What is the ex-boyfriend doing to remain relevant?*
2. *How much value or power does he still have?*
3. *How much harder do I have to work or chase to actually be with her?*
4. *If the ex-boyfriend is so important or special, why aren't they together now?*
5. *Is the ex-boyfriend the standard for future relationships?*

It isn't so uncommon for an ex-boyfriend and ex-girlfriend to move forward in their individual lives and eventually become just friends again, or for the first time. But again, men are observant, and if he knows that someone from the past has the clout he is trying to have, the attention he is trying to have, the longevity he is trying to have, and the affection he is trying to have, he is not going to continue his pursuit. The problem isn't that the new guy can't handle competition. He knows that is going to happen. But he is also smart enough to know that the ex-boyfriend has more familiarity with that woman of interest, and that gives an "ex" an upper hand on anyone pursuing her. If a woman wants a man to pursue her, she has to separate herself from the one who can easily catch her again. The new man knows he's an underdog, but every man expects fair play.

Some men will withdraw

from a race containing "better than,"

to hide neither from competition

nor from embarrassment,

but simply to remain undefeated

in happiness and self-worth.

IV.

THE DIGITAL CHASE

Chapter 11

The Chase versus technology

Let's face it—we live in a technological world now. We constantly are using computers and laptops, cellular phones (smartphones), digital tablets, and other electronic devices. With those devices comes the use of social media. Everyone who has a profile can communicate with each other on several platforms that are sometimes linked up together. There are online dating sites that somehow serve as an upgrade to blind dating. Although it is very useful, some individuals feel that technology, social media especially, has a dramatic effect on how men pursue women (and vice-versa).

#MCM and #WCW

On social media, there is a hashtag for a new phenomenon called "Man-crush Monday," where women post pictures of their man-crush. Usually it's a celebrity of some sort, and just as equivalent, there is "Woman-crush

Wednesday" for men to do the same. What seems to be harmless admiration for someone can easily be mistaken for something greater by an outside pair of eyes. For instance, if a woman posts pictures of male singers as her male-crush every week, she can just easily be expressing her love for music. But, to a man who likes her, yet, who can't sing at all, that may send a different signal. In his mind, since he cannot sing, pursuing someone who loves singers may seem like a waste of his time. A woman must be careful not to let a "man-crush" on social media prevent a man who has a crush on her from approaching her.

You are what you attract

Posting pictures on the internet has become the norm nowadays. As quick as the pictures are taken on smartphones, they are just as easily uploaded for everyone to see. But is seeing really believing? That depends on who is asked. Sometimes what is posted can attract the wrong person, and at the same time, turn away the right person. If a man sees pictures posted that contradict who he is, what he stands for, and who he associates with, that will stop any potential "chase" from occurring. If the pictures posted already give off the notion that a woman is already taken by someone, already interested in someone, or that everyone has equal access to her, some men will turn away because there is no room for them. They will just be another number, another random guy who is trying to win her attention, and that can cause him to get rejected prematurely.

Text messaging

I always hear how text messaging shouldn't replace actual conversation, either face-to-face or voice-to-voice. Sometimes, people are busy, yet in the midst of their busy day, they only have time for a simple text message to say "hello" ask about that person's day. There are also moments when people are in an environment where they can't talk loud, or at all, and texting is more convenient. But just like I state earlier, some people lack courage to ask for a telephone number, let alone call.

I remember moments where I would text a lot, not only because I was busy, or because of inconvenience, but because just like I said earlier, I didn't like my own voice. Not only did I rely on text messaging, but also social media to have conversations with friends, because I felt better knowing they didn't have to hear my voice. For their sake, I never wanted to feel like I was calling at a bad time, so I would just text instead, and wait for a reply. As much as face-to-face contact makes more sense, it should be understood that text messaging is not a bad thing. Text messaging will sometimes disguise tone, and negates having long conversations or the long silence that occurs in conversations at times. If a woman gives a man her phone number, but feels like the man doesn't call her enough, maybe she should see the positive in that. Sometimes, a man is thinking of how precious her time is, and feels that if conversation grows past the text messages, then the phone call will be easier to make.

The bottom line is this: the use of technology can be a gift and curse. As convenient as texting and social media is, it does prevent the face-to-face interaction from happening sometimes. Online dating sites often lead to an actual meeting, but they usually start off through technological methods. For men who dislike the possibility of rejection, technology is sometimes a safe way to not get his feelings hurt. Reading someone's words is often easier to digest than hearing someone's words. Tone is a powerful aspect to what someone says.

<u>*Something to Consider:*</u>

- *Ladies, if your #MCM pursues you online, and wants to have a date with you, do you say no because he didn't do it face-to-face? Think about it, and then think about how an average guy feels.*

As a man, I really don't see any woman saying "NO" if her ultimate crush asks her on a date just because it wasn't face-to-face. But hey, I can be wrong.

V.

THE "SPIRITUAL" CHASE

Chapter 12

The Chase versus character

Ladies, how many times have you been told that you are beautiful, sexy, cute, or any other term associated with your physical appearance? How many times have you been told that you are smart, intellectual, genius, or sophisticated? Lastly, how many times have you been told that you are inspiring, that you personify joy and happiness, that you spark smiles on the faces of others, or that you are a walking definition of what "blessed by God" means? I am willing to think that questions about your physicality trump those about your mentality, and even more so about your inner being. Yet, it is that inner being that really draws people toward you. Your physical appearance gains attention, but your spirit gains attraction.

What is the spirit? The spirit represents our attitude and our character. It's the ability to feel compassion for another person or the sympathy (or empathy) given to someone in a time of need. Sometimes, because we get caught up in the physicality and the mentality of a person, we miss the fact the spirit that person carries from within is the reason for the other two areas to thrive. Our spirit is a reflection of how we live and think (according to our morals and values) and how they stem from what we ultimately believe (according to our faith).

Something about her

Just as a woman's reputation can meet a man before she does physically, her spirit can do the same thing. A person's behavior can spark patterns or habits that do not "sit well" with some people. Sometimes, these habits are not bad habits, but they are just not preferred. For instance, a man is sitting at a table in a coffee shop. A gorgeous woman comes through the door—hair, makeup, high heels, etc. worn to perfection. She is like a model in that moment. In his mind, she is worth approaching. Right behind her is another lady—pretty smile, dressed in sweatpants, no makeup, is wearing glasses, with her hair in a ponytail. While waiting in line, he notices the model-type woman having an attitude about the service, and she curses the cashier upon her arrival at the counter.

Even after an apology from the cashier for the wait, and after receiving her order, she is still angry—so much so that she spills her coffee. While some may think she deserved this to happen, the young lady that was behind her simply gave her own coffee to the angry woman, and said to her "*You seem to need this more than me. Take this, and I will help wipe up your spill.*" The man notices her behavior and now has a decision to make: 1) go chase after the angry, yet, gorgeous woman and risk making the anger worse or 2) commend the second lady on her gesture (which can spark more conversation).

From the man's perspective or personal upbringing, a woman that is too easy to anger or that will curse at him with no hesitation carries a certain spirit in her character that he won't touch emotionally. What happened in the example was that the value he placed in the "gorgeous" woman decreased as soon as her true character was revealed. Furthermore, the second lady's value increased because her character was able to shine through what he initially thought was a lesser attractive appearance.

You are probably thinking: this situation sounds like the making of a fairytale. But let's assume that it was for real. The second lady could have just let the angry lady's drink remain on the floor, could not have cared for her angry emotions, and even less about cleaning it up for her. But perhaps, in her mind, the second woman felt that in was in her *spirit* to be nice to the other woman, to offer her something that could lift her emotions, or brighten her day. Sacrifice shows other people just how beautiful the spirit is truly.

For all we know, the angry lady could have experienced the worst day up to that point, and just needed someone to be kind to her. At that moment, it wasn't about lavish wardrobe, fancy shoes, or handbags, etc., but rather, it was about the second woman's spirit attracting the man, who almost didn't give her a second look. A woman's spirit can welcome the attraction of a man in ways that physicality cannot. It isn't always about the level of intelligence either. Don't get me wrong, intelligence is important, but it should be balanced with a spiritual nature that says she is joyous from within her soul.

Character vs. Costume

To fully understand what "character" means, one must have an understanding of morals and values. Morals are the set of standards that person uses to determine right and wrong behavior. Values are those beliefs that a person carries with them. Values define what is important in a person's life. Together, these two very important aspects of life give basis to why people act the way they do. When pursuing someone, once the layer of physical attractiveness is peeled away, all that is left is the spirit of that person.

Character can sometimes become confused with what I'd like to call, *costumes*. When a person puts on a costume, they are temporarily covering up parts of themselves that aren't meant to be revealed. Costumes also serve the purpose of putting up a front of thinking or behaving in a certain way just to achieve a desired outcome. Some men will fake characteristics about themselves just to remain in good standing with a woman. It's a copycat system. As long as she likes to go to church, or the gym, or simply read a book, he will "enjoy" those same things. Despite his best efforts, he can never keep up that costume for long. Eventually, it will be discovered that he only fit that mold with hopes of winning the woman as a prize. Women are also guilty of the costume effect by trying to win a man's attention. Some men feel that they can't pursue a woman because they don't know who the real version is in front of them.

Costumes are the reason why the people who once had strong morals and values no longer have them. By entertaining and embracing someone who displayed their costume rather than their character, men and women can easily feel cheated or misled once they lose their sense of self. A man can have strong convictions against doing drugs, and falls for a woman who hides her drug use behind her "costume." If he isn't strong enough to resist her enticement, he may eventually find it okay for her to be herself at the expense of losing himself. Worst case scenario, he falls into the same habits she does.

Because men are attracted by what we see, at a greater level than women, it is easier for us to fall into traps once we let down our guard. Some men feel that since "she is attracted to me," that he should relax his stance just a little bit to keep her happy. If her true character was revealed initially, she would never lose his respect, even if he knows that he could not date her any longer.

A person shouldn't have to change their values (if they're already positive ones) just because someone else influences or persuades him/her to do so. If a person was convinced that his/her values (i.e. integrity, honesty, compassion, courtesy, etc.) are positive values to follow, then falling for the wrong character is not likely. But if a person can't remain true to what he/she believe, then that leaves either one open for "spiritual invaders" to come in and disrupt what was a moment of balance, joy, and peace.

<u>Something to Consider</u>:

- *Take a piece of paper and make a "T" chart. On one side label "character," and on the other side, label "costume." Then take all of your likes, dislikes, attributes, flaws, perceptions–physical, mental, emotional, etc. and categorize them. Evaluate both lists to see who you are–not just to yourself, but to the person who has your romantic interest.*

- *Make another chart for that person (to the best of your ability). Now, if you are not familiar with that person, it may be limited information on this chart. But then, compare both lists. Evaluate compatibility and complementary aspects of each chart.*

The goal of this exercise is to give you a view of how your character levels up with that of the person you like or want. You may be surprised that you are closer to that person than you previously thought. But if you are far away, then at least you know where you are from a mature standpoint. It isn't a verdict that you can never obtain the love from such a person as the one you admire. It's a blueprint. Sometimes, we are just a few improvements away, but aren't willing to see the differences, let alone, work on them.

Chapter 13

The Summation of the Spirit

This entire book featured several reasons why men have difficulty "chasing" after women, why women sometimes are unaware of the obstacles men face, and also how both sides need to grow and mature in order to connect better. Men *chase* what looks good, sounds good, and feels good, but are still missing the target. Women open themselves up to being *chased* by the right man, but the doorway to such an adventure is often flooded with men who are not capable, willing, or determined to court women correctly. Perhaps, both sides have been starting from the wrong end of race. Instead of starting from the physical standpoint, or trying to initially pick each other's brain by using silly mind games and hidden agendas, maybe we should have started with the spiritual chase in the first place.

Our spirit defines our character and attitude, shapes our mentality, and re-affirms our faith in God. Our spirit is based on the morals of our culture, the values therein that define us as individuals, but also collectively as a group. When a woman says "there are no good men around," it is because of the history of men who gave her reasons to devalue any potential relationship with men that could form in the future. When a man's only reason to date a woman is because she is pretty, he devalues everything that she can represent mentally and spiritually, simply because his mentality and spirit are not mature enough to see past her appearance. But when we cling to what we believe and build from that foundation, whether good or bad, the results are justified even if they were never desired. Thus, the importance of morals and values must thrive even in the pursuit of love and affection.

Love is a subject that the Bible discusses in so many passages through both Old and New Testament. It starts with the love of God, Our Father, but also described is how we should love ourselves (not in the vanity sense) as children of God, how we should love each other, our spouses, the church, the poor, the strangers, the sinners, the lost, the forgotten, and so on. When we speak of a spiritual chase, this is what we should pursue. Pursuing the love that God gave to us is our first priority. Jesus Christ died on the Cross for our salvation, because God knew we needed Him to reign in our lives. God loved us unconditionally, but knew we needed instruction, direction, inspiration and motivation.

When people sometimes speak about Jesus, or the love of God, it makes some other people feel convicted or unworthy. Still, God loves us anyway. But like any parent, He knows the downfalls we can face, even in the social realm of our lives. We all have stories to tell from our past that may make us feel that same unworthiness and conviction. We all have "skeletons in the closet" that we don't want to reveal. So we continue to let that stuff rot away in the silence and dark corners of our lives. But unfortunately, it doesn't stay there.

Every new romance we encounter is built on the foundation of those before it. With that comes the pain, anger, lust, distrust, degradation, etc. that was present in that previous relationship. We try to smooth those bumpy areas with the thoughts of the happier moments as if those moments were bandages for the not-so-happy times. Instead, we should have looked to God to wipe those ugly moments away from the main roads of our heart, mind, and soul, only leaving the lessons we learned in them. Lessons from those situations should be placed in the hands of the Father, and we should pray for the direction in which we should go. We should work to improve ourselves so that we can be better prepared for whatever, or whoever, comes next in our lives.

The point is this: why worry about chasing after someone or being chased by someone, when we should turn our attention to *chasing after* God. There are no poor <u>definitions</u> with Him, and communication is not <u>blurred</u>. He will educate us through <u>unfamiliar</u> territory and mature us in the <u>familiar</u> areas. We shall fear God, not because He is <u>intimidating</u>, but because He is inviting and nurturing. (Even strict parents love deeply.) God <u>realistically</u> will bring about peace and joy in our lives. He will do just what he promised to do. God doesn't dwell on the <u>superficial</u>, but challenges us to serve Him in the deep inner core of our being. He is there to carry us even we are too <u>exhausted</u> to carry ourselves. Even when things seem <u>uncertain</u>, we can still win the race we're running as long as He is lighting the path. He is not going to run away from us, for He is always there when we need Him. He is the only <u>runner</u> we need in the race with us. We can call him anytime, or "spiritually text" him our prayers and praises in just a few words. He always responds.

The Lord wants us to find love romantically, but He has to organize the race. Women: ask God to show you what to look for in a man, what to accept (and not accept) in a man, and the patience needed to wait on his arrival. Men: pray to God for guidance on how to be a better man, and to prepare you for being the boyfriend and husband. Maybe you gave up too soon in the past, or never began His race in the first place. Maybe those past situations could have prospered into loving relationships, and maybe some needed to end. Maybe some were destined to be just friendships. Maybe some breakups were your fault, and maybe some had nothing to do with you. Whatever it was, or whatever it is now, take it to the Lord in prayer.

Just imagine—if both men and women connect to God by chasing after Him first, the *chases* we endure will no longer be viewed upon as burdens. Instead, because we opened our hearts to learning and sharing, they will be the most beautiful pursuits we ever experience. Pray to learn love. Learn love to give love. Give love to share love. Share love to keep love growing forever.

Some Helpful Bible verses

Deuteronomy 6:5 (KJV)
"And thou shalt love the Lord thy God with all thine heart, and with all thy soul, and with all thy might."

Proverbs 1:7 (KJV)
"The fear of the Lord is the beginning of knowledge: but fools despise wisdom and instruction."

Proverbs 13:20 (KJV)
"He that walketh with fools with wise men shall be wise; but a companion of fools shall be destroyed."

Proverbs 31: 26 (NKJV)
"She opens her mouth with wisdom, and on her tongue is the law of kindness."

Ezekiel 34:12 (NKJV)
"...for with their mouth they show much love, but their hearts pursue their own gain."

Habbakuk 2:2-3 (KJV)
"And the Lord answered me, and said, Write the vision and make it plain upon tables...For the vision is yet for an appointed time...Though it tarry, wait for it; because it will surely come; it will not tarry."

I Corinthians 13:8 (NKJV)
"Love never fails."

I Corinthians 14:20 (NKJV)
"Brethren do not be children in understanding...but in understanding be mature."

2 Corinthians 5:14 (NKJV)
"For the love of Christ compels us...that those who live should live no longer for themselves, but for Him who died for them and rose again."

Ephesians 3:19 (KJV)
"And to know the love of Christ, which passeth knowledge, that ye might be filled with all the fullness of God."

I Thessalonians 5:15 (KJV)
"...but ever follow that which is good, both among yourselves, and to all men."

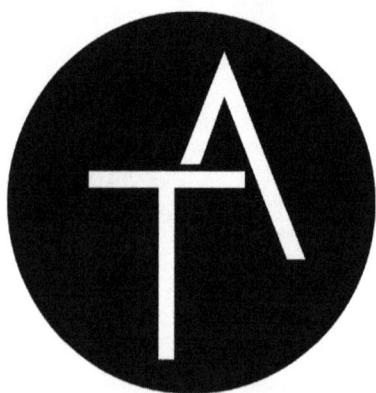

T.A. ACKER,LLC

ABOUT THE AUTHOR

Tyrone Avery Acker was born and raised in Savannah, GA. He attended Armstrong Atlantic State University, graduating with a Bachelor's degree in Radiologic Sciences in 2004. In 2011, he completed his Masters' degree in Adult Education and Community Leadership.

After writing and self-publishing four poetry books from 2008 to 2013, T. A. decided to step out on faith and write his first book combining self-help, love/romance, and relationships between men and women. Thus, *Why Men No Longer Chase* was written. He hopes to brand himself, not only as an author of poetry books, but other books and projects that can possibly better the lives of readers everywhere.

T. A. Acker resides in Georgia with his wife, Erica and daughter, Elise. He enjoys attending church, bowling, sports, and spending time with family.

www.taacker.com
www.facebook.com/t.a.acker3
Instagram: @taac82, @taacker, @ta_theadvisor
Follow on Twitter: @TAAc82, @taacker

www.ingramcontent.com/pod-product-compliance
Lightning Source LLC
Chambersburg PA
CBHW062003040426
42447CB00010B/1885